Creative Ways to Fund Your
Small Business
In Today's Economy

Making Sense of Highly
Uncertain Business Environments

Straightforward Information in Condensed Format

ARTISTIC / BUSINESS SERIES
created by John DeGaetano

ARTISTIC / BUSINESS SERIES
created by John DeGaetano

About the Series

The "*how to*" series is designed to give you straightforward information on a variety of subjects in a condensed format. These books help you be yourself, and guides your vision on the artistic/creative side of your personality as relates to a business setting. Most experts agree that for many art and passion finds it's way into the things we do, however to make it as an entrepreneur and do whatever it is you truly love, the art of business side comes into play… and vice versa. How you treat your business side of things is really the key to success.

About this Book

Creative Ways to Fund Your Small Business in Today's Economy gives you a clearer understanding of the greatest protective challenges an entrepreneur faces throughout the various stages of owning a business are directly related to: Finding and Securing Capital. We'll give you our take on the entrepreneurial culture, and which valuable resources to use when making a funding decision.

Putting the Pieces Together

This guide is packed with information on the safety or risk of various ways to raise money or finance a new or existing business, and in doing so we have assembled not 5, not 10… but 16 methods as an entrepreneur to fund your small business in today's economy…

The never-ending search to find creative ways to fund growth, use capital in a variety of ways. Includes: Financing huge Startup Costs, Expansion, Purchasing Inventory, and Funding current projects related to Operations or Production. Here, we estimate what the risk may be in a changing economic atmosphere. This may mean if interest rates were to rise, a consumer spending change, a recession, product, service or technology shift, travel hesitation, or other foreign issue or uncertainty happens in the world.

All of these factors affect growth, costs, and funding options available to your business.

Includes a well-collected list of "forward thinking" tips and valuable business resources information to help make your business a success in highly uncertain times.

What does Wikipedia say?

Small Business Financing

Small business financing (also referred to as startup financing or franchise financing) refers to the means by which an aspiring or current business owner obtains money to start a new small business, purchase an existing small business or bring money into an existing small business to finance current or future business activity.

There are many ways to finance a new or existing business, each of which features its own benefits and limitations. In the wake of the financial crisis of 2007–08, the availability of traditional types of small business financing dramatically decreased. At the same time, alternative types of small business financing have emerged. In this context, it is instructive to divide the types of small business financing into the two broad categories of traditional and alternative small business financing options.

There have traditionally been two options available to aspiring or existing entrepreneurs looking to finance their small business or franchise: borrow funds (debt financing) or sell ownership interests in exchange for capital (equity financing) explained in greater detail in the coming pages.
*Information courtesy of Wikipedia, the free encyclopedia.

Business Plan – a formal statement of business goals, and plans in reaching them is recommended to have on hand for funding requests. It contains background information and covers a clear understanding and vision of the organization or team.

Business plans may target changes in perception and branding by the customer, client, taxpayer, or larger community. When the existing business is to assume a major change or when funding a new venture, a 3 to 5 year business plan is required, since investors and lenders will look for the safe return of their investment return in that timeframe.

Interesting Facts

Growth and Survival Statistics – Take a look at the numbers behind small business statistics. From success rates, to finances, to deeply concerning government data - hopefully this information helps support fresh ideas for your business plan.

How many small businesses are in the United States? As of 2016, there were 28.8 million small businesses, which accounted for 99.7% of US businesses. (Source: SBA Gov 2016) – Usually less than 7 million in sales and fewer than 500 employees are widely considered small businesses.

What stops small businesses from growing and surviving? The greatest challenge to small business growth and survival is economic uncertainty, followed closely by lower consumer spending and regulatory burdens. (Source: (NSBA) National Small Business Association)

What percentage of U.S. businesses are home-based? As of 2014, 52% of U.S. businesses were home-based. (Source: SBA 2014)

Do banks approve small business loans? Believe it or not... Big banks only approved around 24.1% of small business loans. Smaller banks have a much higher approval rate of around 48.9%. Alternative Lenders approved 58.2% of loan requests. (Source: Biz2Credit 2017)

How much is the average SBA 7(a) loan amount? The average SBA 7(a) loan is $371,628. The maximum loan amount is $5 million. There is no minimum. (Source: (SBA) U.S. Small Business Administration 2017)

How much capital is needed to start a small business? 64% of small business owners start with $10,000 or less, and are primarily self-funded. (Source: Intuit 2014)

What percentage of small businesses are self-financed? 75% of small businesses used their own personal finances as primary startup funding. Other funding options were banks at 16% and family/friends at 6%. (Source: BlueVine 2015)

"The latest government travel data is deeply concerning. For anyone who cares about the economic well-being of the United States,"

said Roger Dow, CEO and president of the US Travel Association. The 3.9 percent decline is steeper than anticipated. Perhaps the most troubling part of the new Department of Commerce data is that much of the decline in international arrivals comes from countries that are vital for US tourism.

"Travel is our country's number two export and supports more than 15 million Americans."

The decline includes a 5.7 percent reduction in overseas arrivals, and a decrease of 9.4 percent from Mexico. (Source: travel.trade.gov) This is just one example of how world issues can affect economic impact, planning, financing, and growth.

Statistics and Growth

General Business Statistics
As a business owner, you will need a solid understanding of your market and current economic conditions to plan for business growth and success. The SBA Dept at sba.gov has a wealth of information to help you indentify your market and demographic information. The following resources provide statistics and reports on a variety of U.S. industries and business conditions (information courtesy of the SBA Dept.)

North American Industry Classification System (NAICS Codes) – Provides the standard used by Federal statistical agencies in classifying business establishments for the purpose of collecting, analyzing and publishing statistical data related to the U.S. business economy. Information includes definition of each industry and background material.

FedStats – Offers a full range of official statistical information produced by more than 100 agencies. Site provides data and trend information on topics such as economic and population trends, crime, education, health care, aviation safety, energy use, farm production and more.

Statistical Abstract of the United States – Presents an authoritative and comprehensive summary of statistics on the social, political and economic conditions in the United States.

Statistics of U.S. Businesses – Features a collection of data files created from U.S. Census County Business Patterns, an annual series that provides sub-national economic data by industry.

Economic Impact. Based on their records, the U.S. Bureau of Labor and Statistics summarizes a business chief goal is to attract, motivate and retain the most qualified employees and match them to jobs for which they are best suited. This translates into dollars and cents… ultimately, Economic Impact through reputation, planning, and growth.

Let's Set The Stage

Tech and The Economy Just 20 Years Ago…

- The Search Engine Google is founded
- Apple Computer unveils the iMac
- U.S. Bancorp lowers its prime rate to 8.25%
- Worlds first Digital Terrestrial Television Service is launched
- Windows 98 released by Microsoft in June
- US Dept. of Justice brings Anti-Trust Case against Microsoft
- Technology starts to mature as E-commerce takes off

- Average Yearly Income $38,100, Average Monthly Rent $619.00

The World, Cost of Living, Etc.
Just 20 Years Ago...

- 19 European nations agree to forbid human cloning
- Bill Clinton Impeached for perjury and obstruction of justice
- India and Pakistan test nuclear weapons
- The FDA approves Viagra for use
- Average cost of new car $17,200
- Average Cost of new house $129,300
- Cost of a gallon of Gas $1.15
- Dozen Eggs 88 cents and 1 LB of Bacon $2.53
- US Postage Stamp 32 cents
(Source: thepeoplehistory.com)

For the NOW – A mix of Good, Bad, and Ugly

- Anti-immigration efforts effect workforce and Tax concerns
- The potential of a trade war and/or foreign policy concerns
- Incomes are rising and true well-being even more so
- Interest rates and inflation remain low
- Labor markets are tight, rising wages puts pressure on profits
- Exports and business investment is picking up
- There is a population shift to the west and south
- Housing will constrain growth in some areas
- Recent natural disasters effect economic pace
(Source: beaconeconomics.com)

Running a Business is Not an Easy Gig

Business owners asked about running a Small business:

- 59% said its harder to run a business NOW, 30% said the same, 12% said THEN
- Small businesses who think its harder point to: 55% because of the economy, 49% said keeping pace with technology, and 40% said more competition

Three biggest difference in doing business THEN vs. NOW

- 84% Use more online marketing tools, 59% said economic uncertainty, 27% said use more automated solutions

So then, forward thinking is more important than ever... That in mind, we'll cover the following guidelines:

This Condensed Guide – addresses the most common ways to finance your business, along with some important tips that you should keep in mind. It is written specifically for small to mid-sized business owners who have passion for what they do and appreciate a time-saving overview key points to available funding options. While their businesses may be different, there is however one thing in common: they all had to raise money to finance their company – to get the business off the ground and to cover corporate expenses.

The Basics – Debt vs. Equity

There are two basic ways to finance a small business: debt and equity.

Debt – a loan or line of credit that provides you a set amount of money that has to be repaid within a specific period of time. Loans may be secured by assets and also a personal guarantee, that means that the lender can take recourse on the assets if you don't pay. A loan can also be unsecured, with no specific asset attached to the loan.

Equity – the selling a part of your business, also known as an equity stake in the business. In this case, you don't usually have to pay back the investment because the new owner of that equity gets all benefits, voting rights, and cash flow associated with that equity stake or a variation of this based on the agreement.

The best solution for you and your business depends on your specific requirements and goals; so all financing solutions consist of debt, equity, or a combination of both.

Short-term Debt
Used to meet short-term needs, such as seasonal inventory or short-term liquidity problems. Repayment: One year or more.

Intermediate Debt
Used for permanent working capital equipment acquisition. Repayment: Three to seven years.

Long-term Debt
Used for real-estate purchases or the initial purchase of a business. Repayment: Seven years or more.

The Business Environments

Overall Economic Uncertainty Risk =

Low Moderate High

What's included for each funding option? – Our assessment is based on several factors, including the rate or cost of the funding option, general long term risk for the business owner, consumer spending risks that affect revenue, such as potential travel hesitation to include international uncertainty, and the fiscal complexity of other conditions subject to creating a negative business atmosphere.

Understanding rating levels is not rocket science, it basically estimates what the risk may be in a changing economic atmosphere. This may mean if interest rates were to rise, the impact on the business would be low,

16

moderate, or high for that funding option. Consumer spending change is also a factor such as the onset of a recession or product, service or technology shift. There may be travel hesitation as a result of a foreign issue or uncertainty in the world. Inflation also changes funding rates making the cost of doing business potentially much higher. All of these factors affect growth, development, costs, and funding options available to your business.

Getting a traditional bank or even an SBA loan to start a new business isn't easy unless you're in business being profitable for at least two years. Luckily now entrepreneurs more than ever have many options to fund their business dreams and some are often less difficult to secure and can be less expensive than a traditional bank loan.

But as a startup, your business a wide range of obstacles to get thing up and running from renting office space, or warehouse location, improvements, etc to buying goods and hiring... it takes money. Ok then with that said, it's time to get to work to get that funding! Below are 16 unique ways to get money to fund your small business:

1. Crowdfunding

Crowdfunding – There are now dozens of services that can help you raise small amounts of capital online. Crowdfunding services allow entrepreneurs to ask friends, family members and others within their online communities for financial contributions to their business. They have become very popular with inventors, entrepreneurs and the general public for many years now. They also allow you to share your company's fundraising story with your friends and family in a less awkward manner than if you approached them in person. Kickstarter is probably the most recognizable, but Indiegogo is gaining in popularity, along with RocketHub, Fundable and Fundly. Others include Peerbackers.com and Profounder.com. Each has its own pros and cons, so it's best to fully investigate the details associated with each site.

Kickstarter, for example is an excellent way to raise capital, introduce a product to market, garner feedback, fund your first large scale production run, and build advance interest in a product or gain grass roots support. Getting the money up front can be a big deal.

Recently, Indiegogo began offering fundraising campaigns without end dates, while RocketHub allows you to keep all the money you raised, even if you don't meet your goal. Fundly is known for its success in helping non-profits, and Fundable is considered small business-friendly. In the end, the right platform for you will be based on your needs and goals.

Rewards-based crowdfunding allows a business to offer incentives to individuals who invest in its company, while equity crowdfunding gives businesses the opportunity to provide a large number of investors a small amount of equity in their companies through similar online mediums.

Keep in mind this isn't about long-term funding. Rather, it's supposed to facilitate the asking for and giving of support for single, one-off ideas. Usually, project-creators offer incentives for pledging, such as if you give a new product developer $20, you may get a sample of that item in return.

In Review:
Crowdfunding services allow entrepreneurs to ask friends, family members and others within their online communities for financial contributions to their business.

- Allows you to share your fundraising story with friends and family in a less awkward manner than in person.
- Kickstarter is probably the most recognizable, however Indiegogo has gained in popularity, along with GoFundMe, RocketHub, Fundable and Fundly.
- Some offer fundraising campaigns without end dates, while others allows you to keep all the money you raised, even if you don't meet goal.

- Some are known for helping non-profits or considered small business-friendly.
- Each has its own pros/cons, so it's best to fully investigate the details associated with each site.

Potential Economic Uncertainty Risk = Low

Economic Conditions that may impact this funding option: Crowdfunding has had a positive affect on small business and offers individuals a chance at success, by showcasing their businesses and projects to the entire world. Under the current economic conditions, this funding option can expand market participation, increase funding access for individuals, draw awareness and funding to neglected issues, and can improve social engagement.

Our Take on the Entrepreneurial Culture: The problem in the crowdfunding context is that the IRS is likely to view it as purely a business transaction and could be taxable (Form 1099-K). On another note, there's no long-term return on investment for supporters and no ability to write off donations for tax purposes.

2. Angel Investors

Angel Investors stand out from other types of funding options because they are always on the lookout for the next business or idea to invest in. They can be private individuals or small groups of executives who invest in businesses, usually by making an equity purchase. They can provide money, expertise, and guidance to help start and grow a business. Many of the biggest tech companies today, including Apple, Google and Yahoo, were funded by angel investors.

Start your company because you are truly passionate about your idea and not because you want to cash in on the latest trend? Angels can spot the difference from get-rich-quick schemes. Getting an angel investment can be very difficult because the investor needs to see growth potential and a viable business plan with a reasonable time span and an exit strategy.

Adding experience on your management team will help ease an investor's fear about your company's ability to deal with a tough economy. Even an unpaid, but highly experienced adviser could add to your credibility. Angel investors and any related transactions must be registered with the Securities and Exchange Commission (SEC). Most angel investments have a time horizon of three to five years.

You'll need all your financials, market analysis, sales planning, etc to demonstrate a good working knowledge of the market they are about to enter as well. Communication is also helpful to keep the investor updated on progress

It's very important that you retain a specialized attorney and possibly a CPA to help you understand how to structure the equity sale; otherwise, you could end up with a substantially diluted ownership stake at subsequent fundings. You can find angel investors at: Angel Capital Association.

In Review:

Angel Investors are private individuals or small groups of executives who invest in businesses, usually by making an equity purchase. They can provide money, expertise, and guidance to help start and grow a business.

- They can provide money, expertise, and guidance to help start and grow a business
- They need to see growth potential and a viable business plan with a reasonable time span and an exit strategy.
- Adding experience on your management team will help ease an investor's fear about your company's ability to deal with a tough economy.
- Any transaction related to investment must be registered with the Securities and Exchange Commission (SEC).
- You'll need all your financials, market analysis, sales planning, etc to demonstrate a good working knowledge of the market they are about to enter as well.
- It's very important that you retain a specialized attorney and a CPA to help you understand how to structure the equity sale.

Potential Economic Uncertainty Risk = Moderate

Economic Conditions that may impact this funding option: Angel investment has boosted economic activity and entrepreneurship development. In fact, as long as the traditional financing such as bank loans became more complex to attract businesses, the development of the alternative investor has become a big topic.

Our Take on the Entrepreneurial Culture: Angel investors are eyes wide-open risk takers with an average of more than 11 percent of their portfolio yielding a positive return.

3. Venture Capitalists

Venture Capitalists, similar to angel investors have money to invest in young, up-and-coming businesses with a high potential for growth and monetary returns. Venture capitalists typically look for a share of equity in exchange for their investment, but are also interested in having a voice in the direction of the company. VCs are looking to make money on their investments, and many feel the best way to do this is to have some control in how the company is managed.

There are a variety of sources available to entrepreneurs that provide for the raise of capital in exchange for partial ownership in the business. Obtaining equity financing, for example from these sources is highly competitive and requires a great deal of vetting from the investor so it requires that a business have a high probability of rapid growth as well as a committed, intelligent business management team. However, an entrepreneur who is successful in raising capital through this method has ample time to repay the investment if necessary.

An entrepreneur seeking capital from this funding source must prepare and understand sound financial documentation and a concrete business plan, and also needs to be prepared to lose some control over day-to-day operations. When financing is provided, business owners must agree to give up a portion of their ownership stake and may even be required to place a member of the venture capital firm or angel investor group in a position on the board of directors.

Young, ambitious and willing entrepreneurs at times make a bet by pledging some of their future earnings. Through an online marketplace, like the Thrust Fund, businesses can offer up a percentage of future lifetime earnings in exchange for upfront, undesignated venture funding. Some businesses are willing to swap 5 percent of her future lifetime earnings for $500,000. Others negotiate other terms however businesses should understand the risk, legality, and enforceability of these "personal investment contracts" which have yet to be established.

In Review:
Venture capitalists typically look for a share of equity in new, up-and-coming businesses with high potential for growth and monetary returns in exchange for their investment. They may also be interested in having a voice in the direction of the company.

- Obtaining equity financing, for example from these sources is highly competitive and requires a great deal of vetting from the investor.
- Requires a business have a high probability of rapid growth with a well-committed, intelligent business management team.
- Entrepreneur must prepare sound financial documentation and a concrete business plan, and also may need to consider the loss of some control over day-to-day operations.

- An online marketplace, like the Thrust Fund, businesses can offer up a percentage of future lifetime earnings in exchange for upfront, undesignated venture funding.
- Businesses should understand some the risks for this funding option in addition to legality, and enforceability of any venture capital agreement.

Potential Economic Uncertainty Risk = Moderate
Economic Conditions that may impact this funding option: From research and development to employment to simple revenue, the companies funded by venture capital are a major part of the U.S. economy. VC-backed companies have become major employers as well. Since 1974, a quarter of net job growth for publicly listed corporations has come from VC-backed companies, however that has lowered over time. (Source: gsb.stanford.edu)

Our Take on the Entrepreneurial Culture: Now, venture capital financing is the exception, not the norm, among start-ups. Historically, only a tiny percentage (fewer than 1%) of U.S. companies have raised capital from VCs. And the industry is contracting according to the National Venture Capital Association (NVCA).

4. Small Business Administration Loans

SBA Loans. The U.S. government has a vested interest in the continued growth and success of the small business sector. As a result, the Small Business Administration offers many different loan types to help entrepreneurs get started. Explore the different SBA loan options here. If your business is a non-profit or educational institution, you might also want to explore SBA grants.

Banks can be reluctant to take any chances with their money because of various economic issues of the past, so loans guaranteed by the U.S. Small Business Administration have become popular. Securing loans backed by the SBA are open to any small business, but there are a number of qualifications, including:

- Under law, the SBA can't guarantee loans to businesses that can obtain the money they need on their own. So you have to apply for a loan on your own from a bank or other financial institution and be turned down.
- In order to qualify as a small business, your firm needs to meet the government's definition of a small business for your industry. Your business may need to meet other criteria depending on the type of loan.
- After determining that your business meets the qualifications, you need to apply for a commercial loan from a financial company that processes SBA loans since the SBA doesn't provide loans directly. The bank's qualifications can be more stringent.
- The technical assistance they provide makes this program a great alternative for small business owners.

SBA Microloan Program is a little-known but extremely helpful program that provides business loans for up to $50,000 to small businesses. Loans are not provided directly but instead use intermediaries to fund the loans.

Many of these intermediaries also provide management assistance and may require training as a condition for a loan. The advantage of this program is that training and assistance often increases chances of success.

In Review:
Small Business Administration offers many different loan types to help entrepreneurs get started. Banks, reluctant to take any chances because of various past economic issues offer loans guaranteed by the SBA. SBA Loans are open to any small business, with qualifications, including:

- Under SBA law, businesses must first apply for a loan from a bank or other financial institution and be turned down.
- To qualify as a small business, firms need to meet the government's definition of a small business for your industry and/or meet other criteria depending on the type of loan.
- Businesses apply for a commercial loan from a financial company that processes SBA loans since the SBA doesn't provide loans directly.
- SBA Microloan Program is a little-known but extremely helpful program that provides business loans for up to $50,000 to small businesses.
- Intermediaries are used to fund the loans and many also provide management assistance and may require training as a condition for a loan that often increases chances of success.

Potential Economic Uncertainty Risk = Moderate
Economic Conditions that may impact this funding option: The business cycle's impact on the volume of SBA guarantees is not clear. When the economy is growing, demand for SBA loan guarantees can increase as small business expands to take advantage of

opportunities or small businesses might reduce their demand because they can obtain loans without the SBA's guarantee. In an expanding economy, lenders are more willing to make loans on more favorable terms.

Our Take on the Entrepreneurial Culture: In economic slowdowns, concern over potential losses leads lenders to tighten all loan standards, perhaps affecting small businesses disproportionately. The demand for SBA loan guarantees can increase as small businesses are unable to obtain loans without the government's backing or interest in SBA loan guarantees can fall because there are fewer reasons to borrow. (Source: everycrsreport.com)

- The average SBA 7(a) loan is $371,628. The maximum loan amount is $5 million. There is no minimum. (Source: (SBA) U.S. Small Business Administration 2017)

5. Microloans

Microloans are really for that startup entrepreneur or an entrepreneur in an existing business facing a capital gap. However, the lack of a credit history, collateral or the inability to secure a loan through a bank doesn't mean no one will lend to you. One option would be to apply for a microloan, a small business loan usually ranging from $500 to $50,000. Microloans are often so small that commercial banks can't be bothered lending the funds.

Instead of a bank, businesses to turn to a microlender, a non-profit organization that works differently than banks. Microlenders offer smaller loan sizes, usually require less documentation than banks, and often apply more flexible underwriting criteria. There are a few hundred microlenders throughout the U.S. and they often charge slightly higher interest rates for loans than banks.

Also available for non-profit organizations, microloans are granted by institutions to individuals who would not normally qualify for a traditional bank loan. Instead of gifting a donation to the non-profit organization, microloan organizations allow individuals to invest in economic opportunities. Microloans are very popular in small and developing nations as well.

AEO represents 400 mostly non-profit microlenders and microenterprise organizations. It provides members with a forum, information, and a voice to promote enterprise opportunity for people and communities with limited access to economic resources.

Accion - is on of the largest microfinance and small business lending networks in the US and has offices in each state. In a sense, they are similar to an SBA Microloan. They provide startup financing and they also fund ongoing concerns. To qualify for general financing, you need to have been in business for six months and you must have sufficient cash flow to repay the debt, among other requirements. Accion also offers startup loans of up to $10,000. (Source: inc.com)

In Review:
Microloans are really for the startup entrepreneur or existing business that faces a capital gap and may have a lack of credit history, collateral or the inability to secure a loan through a bank: a small business microloan usually

ranging from $500 to $50,000. Microloans are often so small that commercial banks can't be bothered lending the funds.

- Instead of a bank, businesses to turn to a microlender, a non-profit organization that works differently than banks.
- Microlenders offer smaller loan sizes, usually require less documentation than banks, and apply more flexible underwriting criteria.
- There are a few hundred microlenders throughout the U.S. and often charge slightly higher interest rates for loans than banks.
- AEO represents non-profit microlenders and microenterprise organizations, providing members with information for people and communities with limited access to economic resources.
- Accion is one of the largest microfinance lending networks in the US. Similar to an SBA Microloan, they provide financing for start-ups in business for at least six months and have sufficient cash flow to repay.

Potential Economic Uncertainty Risk = Moderate
Economic Conditions that may impact this funding option: The growth of the local economies in all the places that micro lending occurs leads to the expansion of the domestic economy. This growth, while only occurring on a small scale, eventually accumulates into real, sustained growth for the United States as a whole. (Source: vedc.org)

Our Take on the Entrepreneurial Culture: When a microloan is extended to a borrower who starts a restaurant in a town, jobs are created, revenue is generated, taxes are collected, and the local economy of that town grows. In towns and cities throughout the United States, small businesses are being created with the help of microloans, a great source of funding for small companies, especially those that have strong local roots within their communities.

6. Personal Financing

Personal Financing. Start-ups can be risky business, so in many cases this level of risk is what prevents traditional lenders from approving loans to entrepreneurs. Perhaps the easiest way to finance a business is to use your own money. In an ideal world, you should save money for a period of time and use to fund your business. This is probably the wisest, most conservative, and safest way to start a company. However, an obvious problem with this type of financing is that you are limited by the amount of money you can save.

It's even more difficult if the startup owner hasn't invested any of his or her own money and even harder to get a third party to give you money for your idea or business if you didn't use any of your own. If you have savings or own your home and are willing to refinance or take out a second mortgage, then these are options you should definitely explore if you're comfortable with the potentially bad consequences.

Some entrepreneurs take this a step further and take money out of their homes (through a home equity line of credit), their retirement plans, or insurance policies and use those funds to run their businesses. This is a very risky strategy because, if the business fails, you stand to lose your house, retirement, and your insurance. And given that many small businesses fail in the first five years, the odds are stacked against you.

In more detail, you can tap into the 401(k) you've accumulated over the years if you're unemployed and thinking about starting your own business. And thanks to provisions in the tax code, you actually can tap into them without penalty if you follow the right steps. The steps are simple enough, but legally complex, so you'll need someone with experience setting up a C corporation and the appropriate retirement plan to roll your retirement assets into. Remember that you're investing your retirement funds, which means you're risking the loss of your nest egg and business if things don't work out.

In Review:

Start-ups can be risky business, so in many cases this level of risk is what prevents traditional lenders from approving loans to entrepreneurs. Perhaps the easiest way to finance a business is to use your own money.

- In an ideal world, you should save money for a period of time and use to fund your business.
- If an owner hasn't invested any of his or her own money it's even harder to get a third party to give you money for your idea or business.
- If you have savings or own your home and are willing to refinance or take out a second mortgage, then these are options you should definitely explore.

- You can tap into the 401(k) you've accumulated over the years if you're unemployed and thinking about starting your own business.
- The steps are simple enough, but legally complex, so find someone with experience setting up a C corporation and the appropriate retirement plan to roll your retirement assets into.

Potential Economic Uncertainty Risk = $\boxed{\text{Low}}$

Economic Conditions that may impact this funding option: Using your own money to finance your business is the easiest way to start a business, however it may put an immediate strain on you and your family's finances based current economic status. Several factors to consider is the cost of self-funding the business, the state of the local economy when established and the long term risk as a business owner, and other conditions that may have a negative impact on growth.

Our Take on the Entrepreneurial Culture: Saving to start or operate a business is a great idea. However, it's not advisable to use retirement savings, home loans, insurance loans, and similar sources to finance risky business ventures. You should consider speaking to a qualified financial advisor if you plan to do so.

- 64% of small business owners start with $10,000 or less, and are primarily self-funded. (Source: Intuit 2014)

7. **Purchase Order Financing**

Purchase Order Financing. Many different factors can affect a business and cash flow, including seasonality of supply and demand. Some businesses can find themselves unable to fulfill large orders due to a lack of funds to purchase the materials needed to produce the product.

Depending on the circumstances, purchase order financing might be a reasonable choice. Purchase order financing organizations extend an advance to the organization based on purchase order amounts. The business can then utilize the funds in advance to purchase the materials it needs sooner and then repay that amount once the goods are sold.

Ever though the rates can be high, companies that most often qualify for purchase order financing are those that deal in manufactured goods, not services and that stand to make a margin of at least 20% or more on the sale. Purchase order funding can be a great option for companies with high gross margins and whose only problem is a lack of cash flow because of slow-paying clients.

Factoring can provide a reliable source of funding and has been gaining popularity in recent years if your company has cash flow problems because clients pay their invoices slowly. When used correctly, the line can improve your cash status and enable you to take on new clients. Getting factoring is comparatively easy and the line is usually very flexible. Given its cost and qualification parameters, it only works for transactions that have high margins and do not require product customization

However, it can be an expensive way to raise funds. Companies selling receivables generally pay a fee that's a percentage of the total amount. If you pay a 2 percent fee to get funds 30 days in advance, it's equivalent to an annual interest rate of about 24 percent. That said, an economic downturn forces companies to look to alternative financing methods and companies like The Receivables Exchange. The exchange allows companies to offer their receivables to dozens of factoring companies at once, along with hedge funds, banks, and other finance companies. These lenders bid on the invoices, which can be sold in a bundle or one at a time.

In Review:
Depending on circumstances, purchase order financing can be a reasonable choice. Financing organizations extend an advance to the organization based on purchase order amounts. The business can then utilize the funds in advance to purchase the materials it needs sooner and then repay that amount once the goods are sold.

- Companies that most often qualify for purchase order financing are those that deal in manufactured goods, not services and that stand to make a margin of at least 20% or more.
- Factoring can provide a reliable source of funding and has gained popularity in recent years if your company has cash flow problems because clients pay their invoices slowly.
- Purchase order financing can be an expensive way to raise funds. Companies selling receivables generally pay a fee that's a percentage of the total amount.
- Companies like The Receivables Exchange allows businesses to offer their receivables to dozens of factoring companies at once, along with hedge

funds, banks, and other finance companies. These lenders bid on the invoices, which can be sold in a bundle or one at a time.

Depending on circumstances, purchase order financing can be a reasonable choice. Financing organizations extend an advance to the business based on purchase order amounts. The business can then utilize the funds to purchase the materials needed sooner and can then repay that amount once the goods are sold.

- Companies that most often qualify for this option are those that deal in manufactured goods and stand to make a margin of at least 20% or more.
- Factoring can provide a reliable source of funding and has gained popularity in recent years if your company has cash flow problems because clients pay their invoices slowly.
- Purchase order financing can be an expensive way to raise funds. Companies selling receivables generally pay a fee that's a percentage of the total amount.
- The Receivables Exchange allows businesses to offer their receivables to dozens of factoring companies, hedge funds, banks, and other finance companies. Lenders bid on the invoices, which can be sold in a bundle.

Potential Economic Uncertainty Risk = High
Economic Conditions that impact this funding option:
Purchase order payments is taken up-front rather than as portion of daily sales. This can be a major drawback for some borrowers who experience an unexpected dip in revenue in uncertain times. Typically, borrowers receive about 80% of each purchase order – which can put a big

dent in cash flow needs as well. The lender keeps the rest to cover some of the principal and high interest.

Our Take on the Entrepreneurial Culture: This is a short-term solution only. Purchase order financing cannot make up for long-term financing for contracts because they are designed to take care of capital needs for a shorter time span.

8. Vendor Financing

Vendor Financing. Most vendors require payment on invoices within 30 days you may benefit from negotiating longer payment terms with your vendors before implementing late fees and penalties. This could give you more cash to work with in the interim and improve your ability to sell your product.

This takes negotiation and may not be an option for all vendors but is especially important if you have a sales cycle that is 30 days or longer. If it takes 45 days from purchase of goods to sale, you'll never be able to pay invoices in 30 days.

An equipment manufacturer at times will carry your purchase over a period of time thus lessening the load for other financings options and in some cases at a much better rate and term.

In Review:
Most vendors require payment on invoices within 30 days you may benefit from negotiating longer payment terms with your vendors before implementing late fees and penalties. This could give you more cash to work with in the interim and improve your ability to sell your product.

- Vendor financing is especially important for businesses that have a sales cycle that is 30 days or longer.
- Also, equipment manufacturers at times will carry your purchase over a period of time thus lessening the load for other financings options and in some cases at a much better rate and term.

Potential Economic Uncertainty Risk = Moderate
Economic Conditions that impact this funding option: The net effect of any economic down turn or growth stimulus will determine what businesses will pay for acquiring equipment. However leasing can help an organization better manage its cash flow situation in tough times.

Our Take on the Entrepreneurial Culture: Depending on the economy, a lease can keep the asset off of the balance sheet allowing the company to fully expense the equipment or to combine a lease with an eye toward purchase and take advantage of other stimulus options, such as an IRS Section 179.

Grow Market Share

We're halfway there! Here are a couple of tips (besides raising money) that helps get your business off the ground and grow market share.

1. Hire people who know and love what you do. It's not a way to bring in capital, but employees that are passionate about their work usually exceed expectations. Some may disagree, however it can be better than capital to hire passionate employee(s) than secure funding in some cases and then turn around and hire a less interested team that leads to un-productivity.

2. Utilize the knowledge of your financials. Avoid requesting funding from any institution or raising capital from anyone until you develop a comprehensive and accurate way to predict your company's performance. Develop forecasting to include revenue/costs and then compare to actuals on a regular basis especially in a changing economic environment.

9. Friends and Family Loans

Friends and Family Loans. Many entrepreneurs fund their small businesses by getting friends and family to invest in them. Your friends and family have a vested, personal interest in watching you succeed. This might make them more willing to invest in your business. You can ask them to make an equity investment, in effect selling them a part of your company, or alternatively ask them for a business loan, but you have to ask yourself if you are willing to risk your relationship for the sake of your business. And understandably, people are often very touchy when it comes to the possibility of losing money.

Another problem is that when you get friends or family involved in your business you will most likely gain a business partner even if you don't want one. You can count on the fact that your friend or family member will want to be involved in your business decisions. So this situation can affect the relationship, especially if you choose to ignore their advice.

Asking friends and family to make an equity investment can be a good way to finance your company but be sure to get the agreement in writing and have a lawyer draft it for you. Also, you should spend a lot of time educating any investors about the risks of your business. And lastly, just like any other investor conversation no one you should invest money that they can't afford to lose.

40

Ask friends and family for a loan or angel investment. - "If have a network of friends and family with money to invest in your idea, start from there before going to angels or anyone else. Focus on those that are the closest to you and have the deepest pockets. Simply put, because they believe in you. Make sure before approaching friends and family you have a well thought-out formal business plan in place. It makes everyone feel more comfortable about the concept and shows off your seriousness and professionalism. Are you offering equity? Or will this be a loan? Perhaps most importantly, you need to re-emphasize the potential risk involved.

In Review:
Asking friends and family to make an equity investment can be a good way to finance the business but be sure to get the agreement in writing and have a lawyer draft it for you. Also, you should spend a lot of time educating any investors about the risks of your business.

- Friends and family can make an equity investment, in effect selling them a part of your company, or alternatively agreeing to a business loan.
- You should spend a lot of time educating any investors about the risks of your business.
- The investor conversation should include that no one you should invest money that they can't afford to lose.
- Make sure before approaching friends and family you have a well thought-out formal business plan in place.

Potential Economic Uncertainty Risk = Low
Economic Conditions that impact this funding option:
Economic situations that lead to loan arrangements

between family and friends can be complex. Some of the social and financial considerations of accepting a loan from a friend or relative are; Lack of clarity where expectations and written agreements are not specific, Tax issues from insufficient loan documentation can expose your investors to IRS scrutiny which is reason why it is important to have any loans carefully documented.

Our Take on the Entrepreneurial Culture: Borrowing from friends and family is often at a lower interest rate than you can get from a bank. A lower interest rate translates into a reduced overall debt level, which can boost long-term credit for your business.

10. Contests

Contests. More and more colleges, local city and state organizations are hosting small business competition events that allow businesses to showcase their business plan or pitch to potential investors and receive monetary prizes, Businesses can also compete in angel investment events or special grant programs and the prize can be over $10,000. Not only do you have the opportunity to receive a monetary investment, you are also connected with investors who may be willing to help grow your business.

So believe it or not, there are organizations out there that offer these monetary rewards or even financing for businesses and entrepreneurs who enter their contests. Some eligibility requirements, entry fees and judging criteria may apply and varies widely. On the road to building confidence in your idea and your pitch, this might be a great way to get some cash.

A source for a small business owner looking for exposure, mentors or money, entering a small business contest could be your answer. Check out these business contests:

- FedEx Small Business Grant Contest – FedEx Small Business Grant Contest offers a first place cash award.
- Shopify Build a Business – Touted as "one of the world's largest competitions for entrepreneurs.
- US Chamber of Commerce Dream Big Award – awards of up to $10,000
- InnovateHER: Innovating for Women Business Challenge – 3 awards totaling an estimated $70,000.
- Arch Grants Global Startup Competition – competition offers a $50,000 cash grant
- Miller Lite Tap the Future – finalist pitch their business, the winner gets $100,000
- Small Business Innovator of the Year – if you're a small business in New Jersey you can compete for prize money (Source: sfscapital.com)

In addition as mentioned, many state and local competitions also offer a variety of prizes for small businesses, so check out your local organizations and news outlets to see what's available in your area. Do some digging – winning a business contest not only could give your business lots of exposure and a cash-injection, but also lets you expand your network of business peers, experts, and potential mentors or investors.

Startup Competition Guide: A Giant List of The Best Business Contests. Even though some competitions with deadlines that may have passed, some are likely to occur again. Information is available at grasshopper.com

In Review:
Colleges, local city and state organizations host small business competition events that allow businesses to pitch investors, receive monetary prizes and get connected with people who may be willing to help grow your business. Do some digging – because winning can give your lots of exposure and a cash-injection, but also lets you expand your network of business peers, experts, and potential mentors or investors. Check out a few of these business contests:

• FedEx Small Business Grant Contest
• Shopify Build a Business
• US Chamber of Commerce Dream Big Award
• InnovateHER: Innovating for Women Business Challenge
• Arch Grants Global Startup Competition
• Miller Lite Tap the Future (Source: sfscapital.com)

Startup Competition Guide: A Giant List of The Best Business Contests. *Even though some competition deadlines that may have passed, some are likely to occur again. Information is available at grasshopper.com

Potential Economic Uncertainty Risk = Low
Economic Conditions that impact this funding option: Contests lead to collective learning and in most cases positively stimulates local economies regardless of atmosphere. Customer service and relationships are a major element of 21st century competitive strategy. When successful businesses compete it improves industry knowledge and customer emphasis.

Our Take on the Entrepreneurial Culture: Competition drives innovation and quality. Open competition puts pressure on providers to constantly research, innovate and upgrade the quality of their products and services, according to Advanced Micro Devices. If businesses fail to identify emerging trends and changing preferences in the marketplace, competitors can capture market share. Perpetual focus on quality improvement benefits customers and drives industries forward.

11. Product Pre-Sales

Product Pre-Sales. If your business is starting up, launching a new product, or based purely on the selling of a single product, the easiest way to raise the money to produce the product may be to pre-sell it. By pre-selling your product (or offering launch pricing) you can keep expenses down and use the funds to get a product up and running for market. It also gives you an idea what to warehouse to start and keeps you aware that there are consumers relying on you to follow through.

New wineries do it all the time... they'll pre-sell wine club members to build an initial following and customer base. This level of pressure can be a little intimidating for some entrepreneurs, so take time to consider the might be the potential outcome of collecting money before providing a product. To build confidence, you will need to have a solid market timeline in place, pricing incentives, and stick to a specific delivery plan, otherwise customers might demand their money back, which could lead to a variety of problems.

Running a pre-sale may get you better results than crowdfunding your venture alone because people get something for their money and they just might keep re-ordering. So try doing a funding campaign of your own on your website, hosting a presale and advertising it. This way, you could potentially benefit from the traffic and exposure, keep 100 percent of the funding, and pass the savings along to customers.

In Review:
If your business is starting up, launching a new product, or based purely on the selling of a single product, the easiest way to raise the money to produce the product may be to pre-sell it. By pre-selling your product (or offering launch pricing) you can keep expenses down and use the funds to get a product up and running for market.

- Pre-sales gives you an idea what to warehouse to start and keeps you aware that there are consumers relying on you to follow through.
- Take time to consider the might be the potential outcome of collecting money before providing a product.
- To build confidence, have a solid market timeline in place, pricing incentives, and stick to a specific delivery plan.
- Try doing a funding campaign of your own on your website, host a presale and advertise it. You could potentially benefit from the exposure, and pass the self-funding savings on to the customer.

Potential Economic Uncertainty Risk = Low
Economic Conditions that impact this funding option: One of the main factors influencing demand for product pre-sales and consumer goods is the level of employment. Steady income encourages people who are in a position to make discretionary spending purchases. Therefore, the current unemployment rate is one economic leading indicator that gives clues to demand for this funding option.

Our Take on the Entrepreneurial Culture: Prices that are affected by the rate of inflation, naturally impact consumer spending on goods and services significantly. Consumer confidence in the product you're offering is another important factor affecting the demand for product pre-sales.

12. Alternative Lending Sources

Alternative Lending Sources. This type of business loan is a quick, simple alternative to a bank loan. However using alternative lenders might require more due diligence on your part because you want to be sure you are doing business with a legitimate vendor, not to mention coming to terms with a high interest rate. In most cases, these lenders fall just outside of the category of banks or government institutions. Some of the more popular alternative lenders include PayPal, Kabbage, OnDeck, Can Capital, Liberty Capital Group, and Prosper.

Other considerations to take into account; These types of loans are primarily revenue based and require as little as three months of financial activity potential so borrowers can easily overcome common hurdles such as credit and time in business. How does it work? "Collection is automatically draw from the merchant's checking account in daily or weekly micro-payments, freeing up working capital and alleviating the end of the month cash crunch. Terms can range between 3 to 24 months and renewal of credit mid-term, businesses can consider it a line of credit. The main caveat is that these loans can cost more than a traditional bank or SBA loan.

In Review:
An alternative small business loan is a quick, simple alternative to a bank loan. However using alternative lenders might require more due diligence on your part because you want to be sure you are doing business with a legitimate vendor, not to mention coming to terms with a high interest rate.

- In most cases, these lenders fall just outside of the category of banks or government institutions.
- Some of the more popular alternative lenders include PayPal, Kabbage, OnDeck, Can Capital, Liberty Capital Group and Prosper.
- Loans are primarily revenue based and require as little as three months of financial activity.
- Collection is automatically drawn from the merchant's checking account in daily or weekly micro-payments.
- Terms can range between 3 to 24 months.

Potential Economic Uncertainty Risk = $\boxed{\text{Moderate}}$

Economic Conditions that impact this funding option: Alternative lending sources generate economic activity that would otherwise not occur. A significant amount of businesses have some type of constraint that preclude them from pursuing loans from other financing sources, whether due to time, credit, or budget constraints, etc. So short-term funding option can satisfy common uses such as the purchase of inventory, hiring or retention of employees, and the acquisition of business equipment.

Our Take on the Entrepreneurial Culture: Approximately every $1.00 of lending by an alternative lending source leads to approximately $3.62 in economic output. (Source: ondeck.com) Since the great recession, traditional lenders have tightened their credit standards in an environment where fewer small business owners have the cash flow, credit standing, or collateral to qualify thus making alternative sources more attractive to borrowers.

13. Credit Cards

Credit Cards can provide an effective way to finance a business and to extend your cash flow. You can use them to pay suppliers and often earn discounts, certain protections, or other rewards. The downside of credit cards is that they are tied directly to your credit score.

Use credit cards with no or low interest rates, or scrape together all your loose cash, savings bonds, etc. and figure out the cheapest way to fund a minimum viable business or product. Leveraging 0 percent credit cards can be the best way to fund your business since there is no interest to pay in the short term. Beware, through this funding option it may take time to pay off what ever you use and the interest rate can eventually be significantly higher.

Cash advances are another source of funds. Most credit card companies impose limits on their cash advances and charge higher rates for them. As such, using cash advances can be expensive, but they can also be useful as a last resort.

None-the-less, credit cards can be very helpful in extending your working capital and alleviating cash flow problems, especially if you use them to pay suppliers. Be careful not to overextend yourself and remember that your credit score is affected by how you use the card.

Using a credit card however to fund your business is some serious risky business. Fall behind on your payment and your credit score gets whacked. Pay just the minimum each month and you could create a hole you'll never get out of… so must be used responsibly.

Whether you're looking for side-by-side credit card comparisons, info around rewards versus points or you're ready to apply, Nerd Wallet (nerdwallet.com) has gathered everything you need from over 1200 cards in one easy place. See picks for the best cards in every category, rates, compare fees, and redemption rates to help you find the best.

In Review:

Credit cards can provide an effective way to finance a business and to extend your cash flow. Use them to pay suppliers, often earn discounts, certain protections, or other rewards. The downside of credit cards is that they are tied directly to your credit score. None-the-less, credit cards can be very helpful in extending working capital and alleviating cash flow problems, especially if you use to them to pay suppliers.

- Leveraging zero percent credit cards can be the best way to fund your business in some cases.
- This funding option it may take time to pay off and interest rate can eventually be significantly higher.
- Cash advances, another source of "last resort" funds - rate is fairly high.
- Re-payments should be accelerated to avoid a hole you'll never get out of... so must be used responsibly.
- Nerd Wallet (nerdwallet.com) has gathered everything you need from over 1200 cards in one easy place for side-by-side credit card comparisons.

Potential Economic Uncertainty Risk = High

Economic Conditions that impact this funding option:
Credit cards help businesses make smaller dollar amount purchases then potentially generating revenue they might not have received, stimulating the economy. However the interest rates are high so in a volatile economy the cost of repayment is that much more expensive. On the personal side of things, cardholders that incur too much debt, end up having less spending ability, which can negatively impact the economy as well.

Our Take on the Entrepreneurial Culture: Credit cards increase the amount of dollars that a business can spend at one time, thereby flooding the system with both real money (cash) and promised money (debts). Even those who don't use credit cards are affected in this scenario as sellers increase prices based on demand, regardless of whether a customer uses cash or a credit card. Keeping a low level of debt from this funding option helps business credit scores, it also preserves the line of credit for use in the event of unforeseen cash flow events.

14. Peer to Peer Lending

Peer to Peer Lending. The rigid and/or time-consuming procedures of traditional banks have unknowingly paved the way for an industry that has grown tremendously in less than a decade. The peer-to-peer lending industry has become a viable alternative to standard bank loans and is emerging as a competitor to the traditional banking system.

Through a simple online platform, which connects borrowers and lenders, thereby cutting out the traditional banking protocols. The platforms do not lend their own funds but act as facilitators to both the loan-seeker and the loan-giver. The P2P lending system has added much ease to the practice of borrowing and loaning money. Low interest rates, simplified applications and accelerated decisions have made this peer-to-peer model a huge success in the modern world. Having offered borrowers an improved financial landscape, these institutions are gaining foothold and gathering momentum.

While these P2P marketplaces operate on the same basic principle, they vary in terms of eligibility criterion, loan rates, amounts and tenures as well as offerings. Some focus on personal loans and a few target students and young professionals, while some cater exclusively to business needs. There's a lot of information on this funding option, so we've taken more time to discuss them. Below are some of the popular peer-to-peer lending websites:

- **Upstart** - states, you are more than your credit score. On Upstart, your education and experience help you get the rate you deserve." Thus loan eligibility is decided on factors that go beyond the FICO score, such as the school of graduation, academic performance, area of study and work history. Upstart offers loans starting from a minimum of $3,000 to a maximum of $35,000 at an annual percentage rate (APR) starting at 4.7%.

- **Funding Circle** - is a leading marketplace with a focus exclusively on small businesses in the U.S. and U.K. and started the platform to facilitate funding small businesses, as the founders themselves experienced that the traditional banking system was too closed to support small businesses. Funding Circle works towards providing a feasible solution for small business owners and has given out $1 billion in loans to approximately 8,000 businesses globally. They offers loans starting from $25,000 to $500,000 for a maximum 5-year tenure for any business purpose like expansion, new equipment, hiring more people or launching innovative campaigns.

- **Prosper Marketplace** - the first ever peer-to-peer lending market place in the U.S. The platform has grown tremendously since its inception; member base of 250,000 people and has funded over $4 billion in loans. Prosper offers a wide range of loans from debt consolidation to home improvement, short-term and bridge loans, auto and vehicle loans, small business loans, baby and adoption loans, engagement ring financing, special occasion loans, green loans and even military loans. Loans are offered starting from a $2,000 to a maximum of $35,000 for a term of 3 or 5 years, for rates range from 5.99% to 36% annual percentage rate (APR) for first-time borrowers.

- **CircleBack Lending** - offers loans for tenure of 3 or 5 years for amounts starting from $3,001 to $35,000. The APR moves in the range of 6.63% to 36%, and the actual rate that a borrower gets depends upon the credit score, amount of loan, tenure, credit usage and history. The platform is good in cases where borrowers have a good credit history and need a higher than average loan amount. CircleBack Lending offers personal loans for various purposes: credit card refinancing, debt consolidation, home improvement loans, medical expenses, auto loans, small business loans, relocation loans, vacation loans, green loans, motorcycle loans, boat loans and more. CircleBack Lending gives small businesses access to personal loans to individuals rather than as a business.

- **Peerform** - founded by Wall Street executives, is another popular lending marketplace. The platform caters to 3-year loans in the range of $1,000 to $25,000, with annual percentage rates (APR) in the range of 7.12% to 29.99%. Peerform believes that FICO score alone is not an adequate measure of risk. So according to Peerform, it was developed in conjunction with leading economists, their loan analyzer represents a differentiated way to determine the creditworthiness of borrowers, enabling individuals with credit scores as low as 600 to secure funds. Peerform offers funding for debt consolidation, installation loans, wedding loans, home improvement, medical expenses, moving and relocation as well as car financing.

- **SoFi** - is a popular name in the peer-to-peer lending market. The focus of SoFi is to help early stage professionals accelerate their success with student loan refinancing, mortgages, mortgage refinancing and personal loans. SoFi has issued over $4 billion in loans till date. SoFi has a slightly strict eligibility criterion; they look into current or prospective employability, financial history, budget management, job experience, and graduation school accreditation, among other things. SoFi offer loans for much higher amounts; the minimum loan amount is $5,000, which goes up to $100,000. Funding is available for the following: student loan refinancing, mortgages, mortgage refinancing, personal loans, parent loans and parent plus refinancing, as well as MBA loans.

- **Lending Club** - is a premier player in the peer-to-peer lending space. Lending Club is a giant in the online market place that connects lenders and borrowers; the total loans issued till mid-2015 amounted to over 11 billion. Lending Club caters to loans for various purposes like personal finance (consolidate debt, pay off credit cards, home improvement and pool loans), business loans, patient financing (dentistry, fertility, hair and bariatric), as well as for investing. The minimum personal loan amount offered is $1,000 (or $15,000 for businesses), going to a maximum of $35,000 (or $300,000 for business). This popular brand became the first publicly traded online peer-to-peer lending company in the U.S., with its successful initial public offering in 2014.

Potential Economic Uncertainty Risk = Moderate to High

Economic Conditions that impact this funding option: Peer-to-peer lenders may find their advantage over banks becomes eroded as interest rates rise. Credit cards will probably become more competitive (through pricier for less creditworthy borrowers), however peer-to-peer lenders will most likely raise rates as well. So the opportunity to mediate credit mispriced by banks may narrow, particularly in the United States.

Our Take on the Entrepreneurial Culture: Peer-to-peer lending would not have flourished without the benign credit conditions of recent years. Now, with just a click online you can easily apply within a short amount of time without the long process of communicating with a bank, in person or waiting for approvals. Even though rates can be high, you may look at it as more of a convenience.

15. Business Loans

Business Loans and lines of credit are well-known products, in which a bank provides financing to run your business. In a loan, the bank gives you a set amount of money that is repaid over a period of years. A line of credit is a revolving product that can be used when needed and paid back on a regular basis similar to a credit card.

Through these conventional bank loans an entrepreneur who has been in business two years or more has the opportunity to raise capital. But most financial institutions are not exactly anxious letting a business in its infancy borrow funds, even if it's a smaller amount.

Conventional business loans have the benefit of a low, fixed interest rate and can provide an outlet to raising capital but common to banks, it can also require more documentation and more stringent, timely repayment terms. Additionally, if an entrepreneur defaults on the repayment of a loan runs the risk of jeopardizing a valuable business relationship.

It's best to clearly understand and investigate all of the terms and conditions and how the financing benefits your business. Speak with a qualified business advisor, business banker and other entrepreneurs or recommend this guide for different lending sources. Make sure your choice fit your business now and for the foreseeable future.

Lending standards have gotten much stricter, but banks such as J.P. Morgan Chase and Bank of America have earmarked additional funds for small business lending. However you need to make sure your finances are stable before you request for funding and your company has a proven track record of generating cash along with substantial assets. Know your financials and reports that show your business is moving in the right direction. This builds confidence for a lender or investor as to your business path.

In Review:
Business loans and lines of credit are well-known products, in which a bank provides financing to run your business. In a loan, the bank gives you a set amount of money that is repaid over a period of years. A line of credit is a revolving product that can be used when needed and paid back on a regular basis similar to a credit card.

- An entrepreneur who has been in business two years or more has the opportunity to raise capital.
- Conventional business loans have the benefit of a low, fixed interest rate.
- Requires more documentation, more stringent, timely repayment terms.
- Clearly understand and investigate all of the terms and conditions and how this funding product benefits your business.
- Finances should be in order, stable before your request for financing, and the business has a proven track record of generating cash along with substantial assets.

Potential Economic Uncertainty Risk = Moderate

Economic Conditions that impact this funding option: The economy affects interest-rate fluctuations and credit availability and realities that every business must address as part of the financing process. It's best to take advantage of openings in credit availability and lower interest rates when they appear – even if the timing isn't perfect for your growth plans.

Our Take on the Entrepreneurial Culture: In the past, the credit shock of the recession left borrowers unable to repay loans. This is particularly true for riskier borrowers so if the industry were to contract even slightly, those unable to refinance would be pushed to default. If banks were to tighten lending criteria at the same time, small business issues would multiply.

16. Accelerator or Incubator

Joining an **Accelerator or Incubator** is a great way to learn about how to grow a business. Accelerators can be either privately or publicly funded and focus on a wide range of industries. Unlike business incubators, the application process for startup accelerators is open to anyone, but highly competitive. There are specific types of startup accelerators, such as corporate accelerator, which are often subsidiaries or programs of larger corporations that act like startup accelerators.

The primary value to the entrepreneur is derived from the mentoring, connections, and the recognition of being chosen to be a part of the accelerator. The business model is based on generating venture style returns, and process that startups go through in the accelerator can be separated into phase. Some fund cash or convertible debt for a small percentage of equity in your company. They are all over the world, but many are concentrated in the U.S.

Most importantly new entrepreneurs get to learn how to approach and pitch investors, research, access, understand, explore, and analyze data. Being part of an incubator program gives you a chance to listen to insightful off-the-record talks by established entrepreneurs and VCs, as they provide perspective and business advice.

A business incubator is a company that helps new and startup companies to develop by providing services such as management training or office space. The National Business Incubation Association (NBIA) defines business incubators as a catalyst tool for either regional or national economic development. (Source: quickbooks.intuit.com)

In Review:
Joining an accelerator or incubator is a great way to learn about how to grow a business. Accelerators can be either privately or publicly funded and focus on a wide range of industries. A business incubator on the other hand is a company that helps new and startup companies to develop by providing services such as management training or office space. Both are catalyst tools for either regional or national economic development. Accelerators or Incubators are all over the world, but many are concentrated in the U.S. They help participants to:

- Discover; what it takes to raise capital or potential funding.
- Understand, explore, and analyze data.
- Learn everything from pitching to term sheets.
- Tap into a network of mentors, advisors & partners
- Pitch your startup to angels and VCs.

Potential Economic Uncertainty Risk = Low
Economic Conditions that impact this funding option:
Accelerators are essential to the growth of entrepreneurial ecosystems not only because they provide space for innovation, but because they create jobs. It also drives economic growth and fosters an entrepreneurial culture within local communities.

Our Take on the Entrepreneurial Culture: When it comes to how to best reverse an economic downturn, about the only thing you might find politicians agreeing on is the importance of supporting small businesses. The deeper and more involved communities are in accelerator or Incubator programs, the more success startups find and the more impact they collectively create.

****

Business Resources and Related Information

U.S. Census Bureau
Small Business Development Centers (SBDC)
Small Business Administration (SBA)
Business Information Center (BIC)
Women's Business Centers (WBCs)
Minority Business Centers (MBCs)
University and community libraries
SCORE
Trade associations
Suppliers and vendors
Local business mentoring groups
Local chamber of commerce
Local nonprofit foundations
Local or state office of Economic Development
Local credit union or community bank

Business Resources and Related Information (cont'd)
Magazines and newspapers
Business websites and expert blogs
Talking with potential customers and competitor

More on Crowdfunding Platforms
Kickstarter – Most popular – no causes or awareness projects

Indiegogo – Independence – any project, event, charity donations

Rockethub – Raise public interest

GoFundMe – Raise money for donations

Razoo – Hi-tech social marketing, non-profits, donations

Crowdrise – Real world issues, animals, arts, cultures – Charity money

Pledge Music – Music Industry – reward based

Sellaband – Music Artist – reward based

Appbackr – Return on your investment for your App

Crowdfunder – Equity attracting Angels and VC's

Financing Tools and Resources
1. AnnualCreditReport.com
2. CreditKarma.com
3. Wellsfargoworks.com
4. SBA.gov
5. Pitchlending.com
6. Nav.com
7. Nerdwallet.com
8. Irs.gov
9. CDTFA.ca.gov

Financial / Tech Resources
Programs and/or Technology for Banking or
Financial Services

In the Best Interest of the Lender
OnDeck – Chase Bank
Kabbage – Celtic Bank
Merchant Card Advances – 30%-100%+

In the Best Interest of the Client
Smartbiz.com – SBA loan, Celtic
Rapid Advance – Bank Statements
Business Backer – Story Lender
CapWell Funding – 401k Retirement
Excel Funding Solutions – Credit Cards
Opportunity Fund – Microloans, small business

So There You Have It! Finding the Right Road to
Running a Successful Business

Creative Ways to Fund Your Small Business in Today's Economy

Making Sense of Highly Uncertain Business Environments

1. Crowdfunding
2. Angel Investors
3. Venture Capitalists
4. Small Business Administration (SBA) Loans
5. Microloans
6. Personal Financing
7. Purchase Order Financing
8. Vendor Financing
9. Friends and Family Loans
10. Contests
11. Product Pre-Sales
12. Alternative Lending Sources
13. Credit Cards
14. Peer to Peer Lending
15. Business Loans
16. Accelerator or Incubator

Various Sources also include: Economic Trends and Research Data, Conference Board of Canada, and United States, U.S. Bureau of Labor and Statistics, Small Business Administration, Learning & Development Outlook Report, International Workplace Education, Wikipedia, the free encyclopedia, Training Studies, Tested Field Experience, and Trade Associations.

About the Author

John DeGaetano – *on the business side, John is a certified business advisor and instructor and works with many businesses in guiding them in creating economic impact in the form of sales, jobs, retaining jobs, market analysis, and planning. He makes presentations on a variety of subjects.*

On the artistic side, John is the artistic director of a theatre company non-profit organization and author of several full length and 10-minute plays. His stage director credits include; Cats, Pirates of Penzance, Joseph and the Amazing Technicolor Dreamcoat, Chicago, West Side Story, and Evita to name a few. He's assisted with numerous other productions such as Miss Saigon along with Radio and Television work. His plays, informational books and presentations are available on Amazon, bookstores, and elsewhere.

John DeGaetano Productions

More titles in the
**"How to" and "10 Ridiculously
Simple Tips" Series**

Includes:
*Connecting Your Business Plan
to a Modern World
Audition for the Stage
Financial Projections
Marketing
Motivation
Writing a Resume
Sales
Social Networking
Stage Production
Training*